MAKE IT HAPPEN
THE MANUAL

Make it Happen

Author
Denryc Hill

MAKE IT HAPPEN
THE MANUAL TO GETTING RESULTS

Copyright © 2019 DENRYC HILL
All Rights reserved

MAKE IT HAPPEN
THE MANUAL TO GETTING RESULTS
Produced By HolyHood Publishing

MAKE IT HAPPEN
THE MANUAL TO GETTING RESULTS

MAKE IT HAPPEN

Author: DENRYC HILL

This book will motivate and inspire you to come up with thoughts that will give you the confidence to

"MAKE IT HAPPEN"... which is actually the title of an independant movie that I wrote, produced, directed, starred in and edited. Hints the name of my movement.

I wanted this book to be easy to read and right to the point so I narrowed it down to five steps that will give you a boost to get started on your new business venture.

"Get excited!
This is going to be great!

MAKE IT HAPPEN
THE MANUAL TO GETTING RESULTS

MAKE IT HAPPEN

5 steps to greatness

Whats up world, this is Denryc Hill (pron. Denrick) an all around creative that includes being a Movie producer, director, actor plus a music artist and more.

I am also a motivational speaker and now I can add being an author to my accomplishments.

I wrote this book to lead and guide people into elevating their life to the next level of greatness by creating new ways to do business and become self employed by entrepreneurship.

MAKE IT HAPPEN
THE MANUAL TO GETTING RESULTS

MAKE IT HAPPEN
THE MANUAL TO GETTING RESULTS

I was raised in the rough streets of Detroit and I changed my life for the better by cultivating my higher self through discipline.

I know how important it is to share wisdom and help enhance the lives of others that want a good change and upgrade in life. It all starts with a mindset and I'm giving you a perspective from the things I experienced in life.

I ascended from living a life of crime into being a full time entertainer and achieving national recognition by acting and making appearances on TV and in Major movies such as the 2Pac movie, "All Eyes On Me", some of Tyler Perry's shows, "The Hate U Give", "Miracles from Heaven" and numerous other featured cameos.

MAKE IT HAPPEN
THE MANUAL TO GETTING RESULTS

MAKE IT HAPPEN
THE MANUAL TO GETTING RESULTS

The 5 steps to Making it Happen are as follows:

1. **Imagine**
2. **Research**
3. **Plan**
4. **Network**
5. **Test Run**

It would be a great idea to grab a pen and paper and take some notes because writing your ideas will help enhance the vision of you completing the process.

MAKE IT HAPPEN
THE MANUAL TO GETTING RESULTS

MAKE IT HAPPEN
THE MANUAL TO GETTING RESULTS

Step 1
IMAGINE

MAKE IT HAPPEN
THE MANUAL TO GETTING RESULTS

Make it Happen
Step 1
IMAGINE:

Think of yourself doing well having completed your business project and being successful. The more positive thoughts you think, the better you will feel about starting a new business.

Imagine all of the great things that will go right for you and the smiles and appreciation of the people that your business or product services. Generate a feeling of fulfillment within yourself of how your business inspires others and the good impact that it has on society.

Speak to yourself in a good way concerning your business by saying I did it or I can do it!.

MAKE IT HAPPEN
THE MANUAL TO GETTING RESULTS

Along with imagining you can also begin to speak this into existence by setting a few positive affirmations on being successful in business.

One of the things I did to motivate myself is came up with a slogan for my attitude and energy towards being successful... that slogan is "straight to the top with no rest stops" which was significant to me as being an actor. With this mindset and attitude it helped keep me motivated to achieve my goals!

Learning how to relax & meditate is a powerful way to enhance your imagination. I will have a book on meditation soon but for now just do some research and practice.

MAKE IT HAPPEN
THE MANUAL TO GETTING RESULTS

MAKE IT HAPPEN
THE MANUAL TO GETTING RESULTS

Step 2
RESEARCH

MAKE IT HAPPEN
THE MANUAL TO GETTING RESULTS

MAKE IT HAPPEN
THE MANUAL TO GETTING RESULTS

THINK - IMAGINE - SPEAK - RELAX
Make it Happen
Step 2
RESEARCH:

It's best to know as much as possible about a particular thing before you go into business so you will be fully prepared for what it entails. You will need to know things like cost, profits and different places and options where you can get products or be able to provide your services from. Make a list of all the things that you feel like you need to know in order to confidently move forward. Its vast amounts of information online and through YouTube videos. You can learn and see examples and get great advice on just about anything you can think of. Remember to take notes and write out key words and information.

MAKE IT HAPPEN
THE MANUAL TO GETTING RESULTS

MAKE IT HAPPEN
THE MANUAL TO GETTING RESULTS

- Cost
- Profits
- Products
- Services
- Knowledge
- Learn the business
- Study (notes)

MAKE IT HAPPEN
THE MANUAL TO GETTING RESULTS

Step 3
PLAN

MAKE IT HAPPEN
THE MANUAL TO GETTING RESULTS

Make it Happen
Step 3
PLAN:

After researching you should have enough information that will give you input on how you want to plan things out.

Make a step-by-step process that is efficient to the things you need to do first **(prioritize)**.

Be sure to line things up so that it makes perfect sense in the order of what you need to start the business.

Planning is always a great way to get things started. Even if some of the details in the plan change at least you have some guidelines and a organized thought to refer to.

MAKE IT HAPPEN
THE MANUAL TO GETTING RESULTS

MAKE IT HAPPEN
THE MANUAL TO GETTING RESULTS

Be sure to **write it** out or type it up and also maybe even make **voice memos** so you have some kind of record of the plan...

As a piece of advice it would be wise to **email yourself** some of the literature just so that you know you can always have a place you can go back and recover it from.

- **Write it**
- **Voice memo**
- **Back up (email it)**
- **Prioritize**

MAKE IT HAPPEN
THE MANUAL TO GETTING RESULTS

MAKE IT HAPPEN
THE MANUAL TO GETTING RESULTS

Step 4
NETWORK

MAKE IT HAPPEN
THE MANUAL TO GETTING RESULTS

Make it Happen
Step 4
NETWORK:

Talk to people that are already in the business that you aspire to start.

Go to different events and engagements to meet people in that field.

The more resources you have within that idea the more input that will automatically come to you.

You can also learn a lot from the experiences of others.

Keep a record of the people and places that you add to your network. Develop good friendships and or alliances with people that relate to your business.

MAKE IT HAPPEN
THE MANUAL TO GETTING RESULTS

MAKE IT HAPPEN
THE MANUAL TO GETTING RESULTS

Step 5
Test Run

MAKE IT HAPPEN
THE MANUAL TO GETTING RESULTS

Make it Happen
Step 5
<u>TEST RUN:</u>

Set a day and time to get started for your test run. Make a list of prospects which is potential people that will buy your product or service. You will learn a lot from your own personal experience and it will give you some insight on how to improve your work ethics and strategy.

Think of the best places and people to reach out to, to make a sale. Record your input and keep track of your customers and people that potentially want to patronize your services also make notes of things that will help you and getting better. Consistency is key you can do it stay focused.

MAKE IT HAPPEN
THE MANUAL TO GETTING RESULTS

__Application__

- **Set Day/time**
- **Make list**
- **Evaluate**
- **Record input**
- **Push for sales**
- **Stay Consistent**

MAKE IT HAPPEN
THE MANUAL TO GETTING RESULTS

You did it you completed the Make it happen Book

Now lets put in the work in the

Make it Happen Workbook!

MAKE IT HAPPEN
THE MANUAL TO GETTING RESULTS

MAKE IT HAPPEN
THE MANUAL TO GETTING RESULTS

MAKE IT HAPPEN the Workbook
WORKBOOK SECTION

MAKE IT HAPPEN
THE MANUAL TO GETTING RESULTS

MAKE IT HAPPEN

MAKE IT HAPPEN

Now that you have read the make it happen guide to Greatness, I want to walk you through your personal steps to assure you can and will make it.

Thank you for investing in your self by taking the time to learn how to be Great -

You have read the book now lets do the work

This workbook will get you motivated and encouraged

Now lets begin
Make it Happen!

MAKE IT HAPPEN
THE MANUAL TO GETTING RESULTS

MAKE IT HAPPEN the Workbook

WORKBOOK SECTION

Asking yourself these simple yet powerful questions will help you vision the details of what needs to be done and will keep the tasks fresh on your mind.

Writing the answers will program the thoughts and energy of taking action into your mind. "Always imagine getting good results from your actions."

MAKE IT HAPPEN
THE MANUAL TO GETTING RESULTS

MAKE IT HAPPEN
THE MANUAL TO GETTING RESULTS

Imagine

MAKE IT HAPPEN
THE MANUAL TO GETTING RESULTS

IMAGINE: *(with feelings and good energy)*

What will you imagine?

How will it feel, sound, smell etc?

What are some of the details?

MAKE IT HAPPEN
THE MANUAL TO GETTING RESULTS

MAKE IT HAPPEN
THE MANUAL TO GETTING RESULTS

RESEARCH

MAKE IT HAPPEN
THE MANUAL TO GETTING RESULTS

MAKE IT HAPPEN
THE MANUAL TO GETTING RESULTS

RESEARCH: *(to gain knowledge of the business)*

What will you research?

How will you research?

Why is it important?

MAKE IT HAPPEN
THE MANUAL TO GETTING RESULTS

MAKE IT HAPPEN
THE MANUAL TO GETTING RESULTS

PLAN

MAKE IT HAPPEN
THE MANUAL TO GETTING RESULTS

MAKE IT HAPPEN
THE MANUAL TO GETTING RESULTS

PLAN: *(to make sense in every step)*

What is the first step of the plan?

What is the second step of the plan?

What is the third step of the plan?

MAKE IT HAPPEN
THE MANUAL TO GETTING RESULTS

MAKE IT HAPPEN
THE MANUAL TO GETTING RESULTS

NETWORK

MAKE IT HAPPEN
THE MANUAL TO GETTING RESULTS

MAKE IT HAPPEN
THE MANUAL TO GETTING RESULTS

NETWORK: *(to gain resources and information)*

What will you gain from networking?

Where will you network?

Who will you network with?

MAKE IT HAPPEN
THE MANUAL TO GETTING RESULTS

MAKE IT HAPPEN
THE MANUAL TO GETTING RESULTS

TEST RUN

MAKE IT HAPPEN
THE MANUAL TO GETTING RESULTS

TEST RUN: (to ensure efficiency)

How will you get started?

What will you record about your test run?

What are some of your test run notes?

MAKE IT HAPPEN
THE MANUAL TO GETTING RESULTS

MAKE IT HAPPEN
THE MANUAL TO GETTING RESULTS

Now that you have written out details of the formula to your individual goals, here is some extra incentives to motivate you to make it happen!

This is a set of words for you to look up and define to stay in alignment with your visions and goals. Give two definitions for each word…

1st What it means to you
2nd What the textbook version is

MAKE IT HAPPEN
THE MANUAL TO GETTING RESULTS

MAKE IT HAPPEN
THE MANUAL TO GETTING RESULTS

Define

1] Discipline

2] Success

3] Business

4] Change

5] Prosperity

6] Unity

7] Planning

MAKE IT HAPPEN
THE MANUAL TO GETTING RESULTS

MAKE IT HAPPEN
THE MANUAL TO GETTING RESULTS

Now pick 7 words of your own. Connected to you and what your about to Make happen.

1.

2.

3.

4.

5.

6.

7.

MAKE IT HAPPEN
THE MANUAL TO GETTING RESULTS

MAKE IT HAPPEN
THE MANUAL TO GETTING RESULTS

Extra tips to Making in happen

TRAVEL DATA

Make notes about where and why you want to travel as it relates to doing business.

Driving distance?

Cost of airplane ticket, etc?

Gas price, miles and costs?

Food deals, planning?

Hotels, Rooms?

Friends, Resources?

Purpose for going?

What events relate to you?

How long will you visit?

MAKE IT HAPPEN
THE MANUAL TO GETTING RESULTS

Make it happen
GOAL SETTING

-Daily

-Weekly

-Monthly

-Yearly

#Tasks

#Budget

#Ideas

You can always refer back to your notes and revise it with updates and new information.

MAKE IT HAPPEN
THE MANUAL TO GETTING RESULTS

Make it Happen
ASSIGNMENT

{Write some basic notes that will help you in life and in business. Also write a story about past success no matter how small or big… You can look at it at any time for self motivation.}

MAKE IT HAPPEN
THE MANUAL TO GETTING RESULTS

Make it Happen
PERSONAL APPLICATION

This personal application is so you can get to know yourself better and also get you in the mode of filling out paperwork to do business.

Name:
Age:
Birthday:
Height:
Weight:
Eye color:
Hair color:
City, State:
Sizes;
{shirt, neck, sleeve
{pants, waist, length
{jacket
{shoe
{hat

MAKE IT HAPPEN
THE MANUAL TO GETTING RESULTS

MAKE IT HAPPEN
THE MANUAL TO GETTING RESULTS

Favorite food:
Favorite color:
Favorite month:
Favorite person:

Three references:
(have ready be prepared Name address phone email)

Hobbies:

Special skills:

Relationship status/goals:

What places would you like to travel and why:

What business would you start and why:

MAKE IT HAPPEN
THE MANUAL TO GETTING RESULTS

MAKE IT HAPPEN
THE MANUAL TO GETTING RESULTS

Create some of your own personal questions:

1.

2.

3.

4.

5.

MAKE IT HAPPEN
THE MANUAL TO GETTING RESULTS

Make it Happen
SAVE MONEY/BUDGETING

- Figure out best prices for things

- What to cut back on spending

- How to unify your purchasing power

- Track your spending habits

- Less vs More

- Saving strategies… ex. $20 a day 30/days = $600

- Make a budget plan and or notes

MAKE IT HAPPEN
THE MANUAL TO GETTING RESULTS

Make it Happen
QUIZ QUESTIONS

[Writing the answers is a great way to keep business on your mind.]

What are the five steps to make it happen?

What are three good ways to network?

Why is imagening important?

Why should you plan?

What are some things you should research?

MAKE IT HAPPEN
THE MANUAL TO GETTING RESULTS

Now how will you make it happen?

MAKE IT HAPPEN SELF MOTIVATING INSPIRATIONAL WORDS

Read these words to yourself and also out loud with boldness when permitted.
Rewrite the words to program your mind with good thoughts daily!

I AM BOLD
I AM SMART
I AM STRONG
I AM POWERFUL
I AM A GREAT LEADER
I AM SELF MOTIVATED
I AM HIGHLY CAPABLE
I AM SUCCESSFUL
I AM HEALTHY
I AM CONSISTENT
I ALWAYS DO GREAT WORK
I AM CONFIDENT
I AM WISE
I FEEL GOOD ALL THE TIME
I AM AN EXCELLENT MONEY MANAGER
I CREATE MY JOY AND ALIVENESS
I LOVE MYSELF

MAKE IT HAPPEN
THE MANUAL TO GETTING RESULTS

MAKE IT HAPPEN
THE MANUAL TO GETTING RESULTS

I AM

I AM

I AM

I AM

I AM

MAKE IT HAPPEN
THE MANUAL TO GETTING RESULTS

MAKE IT HAPPEN
THE MANUAL TO GETTING RESULTS

You are a person that Makes It Happen.

I believe in you.

Welcome to the Make it happen Movement

Let's change the world for the better together.

Now Go

&

Make it Happen!

MAKE IT HAPPEN
THE MANUAL TO GETTING RESULTS

MAKE IT HAPPEN
THE MANUAL TO GETTING RESULTS

MAKE IT HAPPEN

Denryc Hill is a Detroit native that has established an entertainment career in GA. After transitioning from the street life he has completed several independent movie projects and also has worked on major movies & TV shows. In addition to this he is still adding to his accomplishments! Being have made it to new levels of success, he is compelled to share his story and give advice to others that plan to reach another level of greatness. His new movement is called "MAKE IT HAPPEN" which is an exciting, motivational guide to self improvement! Including A movie, inspirational lectures and a book plus more.

Follow his movement at these internet, social site locations:

Facebook/ Denryc Hill
Instagram/ denrychill
Youtube channel/ Golden Thoughts
Anchor Podcast/ Golden Thoughts

MAKE IT HAPPEN
THE MANUAL TO GETTING RESULTS

MAKE IT HAPPEN
THE MANUAL TO GETTING RESULTS

With this information and details you can apply it to your life and complete the steps and it will surely get you started in business whether you are changing your life by starting a new business or adding a new business. You are already on your way and more equipped just by reading this book, job well done.

"MAKE IT HAPPEN".

MAKE IT HAPPEN
THE MANUAL TO GETTING RESULTS

MAKE IT HAPPEN
THE MANUAL TO GETTING RESULTS

The 5 steps to Making it Happen

1. Imagine

2. Research

3. Plan

4. Network

5. Test Run

Made in the USA
Columbia, SC
10 August 2021